50YEARS
WORKING IN
CRIMINAL JUSTICE

50 YEARS
WORKING IN
CRIMINAL JUSTICE

JOHN M. PAITAKES, PH.D

MILL CITY PRESS

Mill City Press, Inc.
2301 Lucien Way #415
Maitland, FL 32751
407.339.4217
www.millcitypress.net

Printed in the United States of America

ISBN: 9781545612538

TABLE OF CONTENTS

Praise for John Paitakes ix
Acknowledgements xiii
Foreword xv
Introduction xvii
Chapter 1 – Early Education Years 1
Chapter 2 – Entering the Criminal Justice
            Profession 9
Chapter 3 – Further Educational Pursuits 17
Chapter 4 – Criminal Justice
            Career Change 23
Chapter 5 – Governor's Appointments 29
Chapter 6 – Changes in the Criminal
            Justice System. 35
Chapter 7 – Tips for Success for Criminal
            Justice Applicants 45
Chapter 8 – Ways to Secure Employment in
            Criminal Justice 53
Chapter 9 – Professional Development. 61
Chapter 10 – Where Do We Go
            From Here? 65
Some Career Positions in Criminal Justice . . . 75

PRAISE FOR JOHN PAITAKES

"Dr. Paitakes is truly a one-of-a-kind guy and professor. Having him as a professor for a majority of my Criminal Justice courses at Seton Hall University was truly something that I would never forget. I had a late start to my college career as I served on active duty with the United States Marine Corps. When I came to Seton Hall, I was already employed in my job field as a police officer with the Port Authority of New York and New Jersey. I loved how Dr. Paitakes had extensive knowledge in the Criminal Justice system and the way it worked in the various different elements. He always tried to help out the students and guide them in the correct direction in ways such as assisting with resumes, setting the students up with internships, and instructing the class on how to get into the field of Criminal Justice. Sometimes I would be a guest speaker for some of his classes where I spoke to the students on how I was able to get into the field and ways to succeed. I feel that helped out a lot because it shows that one of their peers was able to do it and so are they. All in all, Dr. Paitakes is very compassionate at what he does and takes tremendous pride in it. I am honored to have had him as a mentor and friend."

        – Jason Nielsen, student

"Dr. Paitakes was my student advisor and professor throughout my four years at Seton Hall University. Upon entering Seton Hall, Dr. Paitakes quickly became a mentor and role model to me. The classes that I enjoyed the most at Seton Hall were the ones that Dr. Paitakes taught. Dr. Paitakes was a unique professor. Because he had such a rich and colorful background working in the criminal justice field, he was able to share personal stories that related to topics that were discussed in class, which made class particularly interesting and engaging. In all of Dr. Paitakes' classes there was an emphasis on exploring various careers that could be pursued with a criminal justice degree. He brought numerous guest speakers into class throughout the semester and always informed the class of any internship or job opportunities that he was aware of. The passion that Dr. Paitakes has for the criminal justice field is admirable. Throughout my college years, Dr. Paitakes went above and beyond for me. As a junior in college, I approached Dr. Paitakes for guidance because I was unsure as to what career I wanted to pursue. Through his own personal contacts, Dr. Paitakes helped me secure two internships within the criminal justice field. I am extremely grateful for those opportunities. Those internships provided meaningful experiences that helped me realize my dream career as a criminal prosecutor. Dr. Paitakes is highly involved in the criminal justice system, which is something that I admire and hope to emulate in my future career as an attorney. Dr. Paitakes has always been a supporter of mine and I look forward to sharing my own future professional successes with him as I know he will take pride in my accomplishments."

— Rebecca Starner, student

"I've known John Paitakes for more than twenty years, having first become acquainted with him when he was my adviser in Seton Hall University's Master of Public Administration program. During my time in the program, he was instrumental in exposing me to the field of court administration, a niche area of public administration and the criminal justice profession. His counsel and encouragement was of great benefit to me as I progressed through my career to ultimately reach the highest levels of government work in the New Jersey Judiciary. John served as Assistant Chief Probation Officer for the Courts. His experience and the balance that his background brought to classroom discussions cannot be overstated. His accounts of daily practices in the profession enhanced my learning experience and were indispensable, particularly during the early part of my career. This 'lessons learned' book will engage readers by highlighting some of the key anecdotes of his career and will undoubtedly come to be appreciated by a wide range of criminal justice students and practitioners."

– Giuseppe M. Fazari, Ph.D.; Assistant Dean, Continuing Education and Professional Studies at Seton Hall University

ACKNOWLEDGMENTS

I want to express my sincere gratitude and appreciation to my wife, Linda, for her patience, support, and assistance in editing and formatting the writing of this text. Without her assistance, the composing of this text would have been much more difficult.

I am also fortunate to have a very loving and supportive family. My daughters, Christina and Tanya, have always been major priorities in our lives. In addition, I have been blessed with three beautiful granddaughters—Megan, Laura, and Nicole—and two intelligent and terrific sons-in-law, David and Garry.

I want to also give special recognition to my editors, Kimberley Jace and Pamela Cangioli, associated with Proofed To Perfection. Their superior editing and helpful comments inspired me to complete this text.

A good friend of mine and author, Mike Papasavas (*Three Grains of Wheat*), also offered advice and encouragement throughout the writing.

I am hopeful that this book may serve as an incentive and guide to individuals seeking careers in criminal justice, which is a most worthwhile and rewarding discipline. I hope my experiences can be of assistance to them.

FOREWORD

A s a professor of Public Administration for many years, I am always looking for textbooks written by "pracademics"—i.e., professors who not only know the scholarly literature, but also have many years of practical experience.

Dr. John M. Paitakes, the author of this book, is one of those individuals. In fact, Dr. Paitakes has a great deal of experience in both academia as well as the professional fields associated with criminal justice. He served as Assistant Chief Probation Officer with the Somerset County Courts for twenty-nine years and was appointed to the NJ State Parole Board by two different governors of New Jersey. In addition, he has appeared as a criminal justice consulting expert on various television shows.

Besides this professional experience, Dr. Paitakes, having received his Ph.D. in Human Resource Development-Public Administration, served as a Senior Faculty Associate at Seton Hall University for twenty years. He taught both undergraduate courses in the Criminal Justice Department as well as graduate courses in Public Administration.

Students usually have to choose between "how to" books written by professionals or scholarly literature written by academics. Dr. Paitakes' book gives them both approaches. That is why it is heartily recommended.

— Dr. Naomi Wish, Political Science and Public Administration Department, Seton Hall University

INTRODUCTION

s I completed my fiftieth year working in
the criminal justice system, I felt inspired to
write this book. I must admit, it seems like only a
few years ago (1967) that I began my career in
this most interesting, humanistic field. I had not
planned on working in this field, and it was only
by chance that I commenced this journey. I was
unemployed and had no specific career aspirations. I had majored in business administration
because my father was in the restaurant business,
and therefore, continuing in the family business
was a strong possibility. However, Dad sold his
share of the business to his partner due to some
financial difficulties he was having at the time. I
had heard from a friend that the court system in
the county where I lived might be hiring probation
officers, and thus began my criminal justice career.

I am the son of a Greek immigrant, John Adam
Paitakes. Born in 1910, he emigrated from the vil-
lage of Vafe, Crete, Greece (population: 50). He
came to the United States with his father, Adam

Paitakes, and his two brothers, Gus and Michael, in 1918. They settled in New Brunswick, New Jersey and resided in a two-family house owned by Dad's uncle, also John Paitakes. Dad enrolled in the public school and continued his education until age sixteen, at which time he withdrew from school. He had to secure full-time employment to help in supporting the family. His father was having a hard time maintaining a full-time job. His mother, Irene, had joined them in America, but due to some health issues, she was not able to work.

Dad, like many Greeks who came to the United States, seemed to gravitate toward working in restaurants and diners. I am not sure why so many were attracted to this work. I believe that they prided themselves on their hospitality and *philoxenia* (love of strangers). In addition, *tavernas* and outside cafes were a major source of employment in their homeland. Although Dad was not formally educated, he was a fast learner and a hard worker. He, like many other emigrants, valued higher education for their children, even though they did not have that opportunity themselves. From an early age, as I was growing up, Dad was adamant that I study hard in school and continue to pursue further education. My mother was a stay-at-home mom. With four children and managing the rentals in our three-family home, she was quite busy. After working for others in the restaurant business for several years, while supporting a family of six and also helping support his parents, Dad realized he had to seek other means. He believed that if he could get into business for himself it would provide him with an increase financially. He met another gentleman (of Greek decent) with similar goals. There is a saying among Greeks: "When two Greeks meet, they open a diner." Dad and his new partner, Tom Parlapanides, purchased an existing diner, restaurant, and cocktail lounge, The Spinning Wheel.

At the age of thirteen, I began working as a cashier and busboy, (clearing and resetting tables). I worked after school, on weekends, and during the summers. When I turned seventeen, I was promoted to night manager. My hours were one p.m. until midnight. I had the responsibility of supervising between fourteen and eighteen employees ranging in ages from eighteen to seventy years old. It was an awesome responsibility for a teenager! I maintained this position in the summers during my college years and for an additional year after graduating from college. This position required utilizing a great deal of tact, diplomacy, and interpersonal skills managing such a diverse number of employees of varied ages. The experience of dealing with customers and staff from all walks of life (from sanitation worker to University President) was an invaluable learning experience. Today's society is comprised of people from various cultures, races, and religions. To become successful, one must be able to work with and supervise personnel with diverse backgrounds. This work experience was helpful in dealing with clients in the criminal justice system, because people from diverse backgrounds could be our clients. This opportunity helped me develop a work ethic that has been a significant part of my persona throughout my life.

My career has traversed through the court's probation system, teaching, and state government parole positions. I am fortunate and gratified to have experienced and enjoyed all of my positions in this satisfying career. I hope to continue my work in the criminal justice field indefinitely, and I will continue to share with my past and present students, and with the public, the value and significance of this important and rewarding career choice.

Author's Professional Titles

Criminal justice positions
Assistant Vicinage Chief Probation Officer (retired)
New Jersey State Parole Board (presently)

Academic positions
Seton Hall University Professor (retired)
Adjunct Professor at Rutgers University, Kean University,
Thomas Edison State University, Rider University, Raritan Valley Community College, Capella University,
Union Institute University, University of South Africa.

CHAPTER 1

EARLY EDUCATION YEARS

riminal Justice is one of the most important issues facing the country today. This book isn't just a how-to in pursuing a criminal justice career. It's about the steps I took to get where I am, the perseverance I applied to keep going, and the passion I discovered in this field.

I'll also tell you a little bit of my history and offer some practical tips on how to secure a position in criminal justice—and how to be successful once you land that job.

I attended New Brunswick High School, located in New Brunswick, NJ during the '50s and early '60s. It was a mid-sized high school with a diverse population to include students of different cultures, races, and religions.

As I ascended through the grades, I was merely an average student. My dad constantly reminded me to study more, ask questions, and prepare for college. Further education was of foremost importance to many immigrants coming to the United States from Europe. Even though they were not able to pursue and afford further education for themselves, parents like mine were adamant that their children would achieve the highest degrees possible.

My dad emphasized, from an early age, that I'd go to college. Even though I had three sisters, because I was the only boy, my parents believed that I must be the first to be afforded the opportunity for education. Like many parents during that era, the thinking was that a male would most likely become a bread-winner while a female would be at home raising the children and maintaining the house.

In my senior year in high school, I told my guidance counselor that I wanted to go to college. My counselor asked, "What do you want to major in?" I responded, "I don't know."

"Since your dad owns and works in the restaurant business," he suggested, "you should major in business."

I applied to a number of colleges and was accepted at Bryant College (now Bryant University), a small business college in Providence, Rhode Island, where I would major in Business Administration. After graduating from high school in 1961, I worked the summer at my dad's restaurant and was able to save most of my earnings for college. In September, after packing for the move, my parents and a friend of mine from high school—Allen Fenkel, who also was accepted at Bryant—made the four-and-a-half hour drive through New

York and Connecticut to Providence. (The university has since moved to a sprawling campus in Smithville, RI.)

After unpacking the car and getting me settled in my dormitory, Mom, Dad, and my sister Lynn climbed into Dad's big, black Buick and waved goodbye. Dad's last words were, "Study hard."

As I watched them drive away, I felt compelled to try. I would remember his command because I knew how hard he had worked and sacrificed to be able to finance a substantial part of the cost of my further education.

Living away from home with forty other undergraduates from diverse backgrounds was a new, exciting, and somewhat frightening experience. My dormitory, Barber Hall, was an old colonial house that had been converted to dorm rooms, so it was like our own fraternity house.

As time went on, I became more acclimated to this new way of living. I enjoyed having the liberty to make my own decisions regarding when to go to bed, when and what to eat, and whom to socialize with. There are so many new experiences involved in living on your own.

Attending classes in the college setting was quite different than high school. Selecting my own courses, times, and even professors was a new and exciting change. In the back of my mind, I recalled Dad's words: "Study hard." But although my attendance was good, I struggled somewhat academically. Living by my own clock required time management skills I hadn't fully developed.

So academically, I did not fare that well the first year, and I was placed on academic probation.

Then, because of a college prank (which was nothing criminal) that many students in my dormitory were involved in, I was placed on social probation. Some of the students were placed in other dormitories on campus. Letters went home to parents telling them they were required to make an appointment with the Dean of the College to discuss their child's status.

When my parents received the letter, needless to say, Dad was very angry. "Do you realize the repercussions of your actions?" he shouted into the phone. "I have to get someone to cover my shifts at the restaurant. Your education is very costly."

I felt terrible about my actions and the disappointment I had caused my parents, not to mention the expense of hiring someone to work for my Dad at the business and staying at a hotel overnight just so they could talk to my dean.

My parents spoke to Dean Gulski behind closed doors for about forty-five minutes as I waited anxiously and nervously. To this day, I can recall Dad's words when he and Mom came out of the meeting: "Unless you change your behavior and grades immediately, you will be suspended from college. If you are dismissed, you will enter the Army upon your dismissal. I am paying a substantial amount of money for your further education and working extra hours so that you receive a better education than I."

I immediately felt remorseful and angry with myself over my behavior. I had caused my parents so much disappointment. After they left, I knew I would turn things around—not only for myself, but for my parents. They had raised me with all the positive attributes and characteristics to be a hard-working and successful person, and I had let them down.

This freshman year incident and the fact that my parents had to meet with the dean was a "wake-up call" for me, which—as I think back—was what I needed to readjust my priorities. I immediately resolved to study more, socialize less, ask faculty for extra help, and become more serious about my education. The results were quick: my grades began to rise and my social activities were more tempered and thoughtful.

I had been thinking about joining a fraternity my first year in college, but because of my low academic standing, I did not. However, as my grades improved, I decided to try. A fraternity would help me expand my network of friends and social interactions, as I was several hundred miles away from home. In my second year, I pledged Beta Iota Beta—now Tau Kappa Epsilon—a national fraternity and was inducted.

Being part of a fraternity assisted me in making my adjustment to college, as it provided me with forty other "brothers" and even "sisters" from the sister sorority. I was learning to manage my time and priorities. I was getting better at keeping in mind that my main reason for attending college was to pursue further education.

As my grades and adjustment to living away from home improved, I decided to seek part-time employment to ease some of the financial expenses my parents had to incur. I secured a position delivering pizzas and sub-sandwiches—"grinders," as they were called in New England. I held this job for several months until the pizza owner's delivery car broke down and I was laid off.

I then secured a job on campus with the maintenance department, working three to four hours a day. This provided me with some spending money and meant I didn't have to ask my parents for additional cash. It also reinforced my work ethic, as I had to start at six a.m. most days. I knew that, if a student employee was not dependable while working for the college, they were dismissed. I maintained this employment during all of my college years.

The time seemed to "fly" by, and before I knew it, I was in my senior year and preparing for the real working world. This was a bittersweet time in my life, as I recall. I was very happy to have reached this milestone—soon to be the first in my family to be a college graduate, WOW!—and I was fulfilling my parents' dream. But on a sad note, I would be leaving the new sense of independence I'd found by living on my own. I knew I'd miss being around so many people with whom I had so much in common.

As I reflect back on my life, I realize that college is the only time in life when you are in such an environment. Once in the world of work, you are usually in an environment with a diverse culture, with people of all ages and different stages of life.

On the day of graduation, Mom, Dad, and my godmother, Mary Moundalexis, drove up to Providence in Dad's 1965 Buick. I vividly recall all three of them (especially Mom and Dad) beaming with pride. Their only son was now the first in the family to attain a college degree.

Immediately after graduation, we returned to the apartment I had shared with three other students, packed the car with all my belongings, and drove back to New Jersey. I would live at home until the next phase of my life began.

On the way home, we celebrated my graduation by stopping at an upscale (and expensive) restaurant, compliments of Mom and Dad.

But even as I dined in luxury, I was haunted by a question: "What do I do now?"

CHAPTER 2

ENTERING THE CRIMINAL JUSTICE PROFESSION

n 1965, the year I graduated college, the United States was heavily committed to the Vietnam conflict. Because of the military draft, if you were eighteen years of age and not in college, it was likely you would be drafted—and there was a good probability that your tour of duty would include Vietnam. Although I never considered dodging the draft or moving to Canada, I was not looking forward to going off to a war zone where so many American soldiers had been killed.

My dad encouraged me to work in the family restaurant until I made a decision to either enlist in the military or wait until I was drafted. I was quite unsure what to do. A friend of the family recommended I consider enlisting in the United States Army Reserve, which required six months of active duty and five and one-half years of monthly reserve meetings, plus two weeks of annual active duty at a military training base in the U.S. That sounded like a great alternative for me. In June of 1965, I enlisted in the United States Army Reserve Unit, 78th Division in Edison, New Jersey.

My active duty training was delayed for approximately five months due to scheduling issues. While I was waiting for orders to commence active duty, I worked full time at the restaurant. I was assigned the afternoon- and night-shift manager position, where I was in charge of eighteen employees from two p.m. until midnight. I was supervising waitresses, cooks, dishwashers, bartenders, and maintenance workers. This was an awesome responsibility for a twenty-one-year-old. The employees ranged in age from eighteen to seventy-four, and a number of them had much more experience in the restaurant business than I had.

Dad advised me to be tactful, fair, and firm when supervising employees. This was a great learning experience in management, but also in human relations, because I was working with and supervising people of different ages, cultures, and races. The lessons I learned, including the ability to work with a diverse population, became an asset later in life in my criminal justice positions. I continued working in the restaurant until I received my orders to report for active duty at the military base at Fort Dix, New Jersey in November.

Some of the trainees at Fort Dix were college graduates, like me, but the vast majority of the training personnel had only high school diplomas. It was a major difference from the college setting, where most professors had their doctorates or law degrees. Only a few of the officers had college degrees. However, my philosophy at the time was to follow their instructions during my six months of active duty, and then return home to fulfill my five-and-one-half years of weekend drills and two-week summer camps.

I completed the eight weeks of basic training that anyone drafted or enlisted in the United States Army must complete and passed all requirements. I was then stationed at a supply center for the remainder of my time at Fort Dix. This was like a normal job, eight to five with most weekends off. I completed my active duty in March of 1966 and returned home to live with my parents and younger sister.

Now I was unemployed and unsure of what type of career to pursue. In the meantime, my father had discovered that the restaurant business was no longer profitable for him. His partner was in a better financial position than my father, so he offered to buy my father's share. They agreed on a fair market price, and Dad was out of the restaurant business. This meant that returning to work in the family restaurant was no longer an option for me.

I had enjoyed working in the "people-oriented" atmosphere of the restaurant. I had learned to interact with people from all walks of life, which was a great experience, although the long working hours—including nights and weekends—were not ideal for a single person. Most of my friends had the weekends off, but in the restaurant business, that's the busiest time. I'd had Tuesdays and Wednesdays off, when most of my friends were working.

I was unemployed for several weeks. Mom was happy I was home and not going off to war, but Dad's regular inquiry was, "Now what are you going to do?" He believed I should get a job as soon as possible. I did not want to take any job, because I was so unsure about a career. I knew I wanted work that was satisfying and "people-oriented." I did not want a job where I sat at a desk for eight hours a day.

A high school friend who had been working as a Probation Officer in Middlesex County, NJ said that it was interesting work. You deal with a diverse population; you're in the nine-to-five work week with weekends off, for the most part. This sounded like something I might be interested in. My family had recently moved from New Brunswick, NJ (which is in Middlesex County) to Franklin Township (which is in Somerset County). The county seat was Somerville and the Probation Department, Court House, and county administrative buildings were located there.

I immediately made an appointment with the Chief Probation Officer, Michael A. Stabile, for an interview. In 1967, a four-year college degree with any major was acceptable to be considered for employment for that position. (Today, most states require a degree in a field related to criminal justice, such as Political Science or Sociology, for probation work.)

My interview with the Chief Probation Officer went well; however, this was a civil service position, and under civil service rules, those with the highest scores are offered positions first. Although the department was short-staffed because of a recent resignation, the Chief said that, if I got the position, it would be temporary pending my passing of the State Civil Service exam. If I did not pass the exam with a high enough score, I would have to be let go.

At that time, you also had to meet with the Superior Court Judge. I met with the judge, Victor A. Rizzolo, and was offered a position. Thus began my twenty-nine year career with the Somerset County Probation Department. When I passed the civil service exam, it became official.

My first position was in the Juvenile Division. The department at that time was divided into two sections, and officers were assigned to the Pre-Sentence Investigation Unit (report writing) or the Supervision Unit. I was assigned to the Juvenile Supervision Unit, which was responsible for supervising approximately fifty juvenile offenders and ensuring that they comply with the standard conditions of probation.

It was an interesting assignment and somewhat demanding. I had to learn the criminal justice jargon and system, because I had not majored in Criminal Justice in college. I had taken Sociology and Psychology courses as an undergraduate; I had done well academically in those courses and had enjoyed them. This position reinforced my yearning to learn as much as I could, as fast as I could, about the juvenile and adult criminal justice systems. There were no formal training sessions in Probation at that time (1967), so most information was learned on the job. Mentoring by longer-term officers and staff was also quite helpful.

The number of Probation Officers when I first started was nine. Shortly after I was hired, the county experienced a surge in population, as many families were seeking a move to less densely populated areas—such as Somerset County. As the population and housing increased, so did crime. Therefore, more probation services were needed, and there was a significant hiring increase. The department began expanding from nine staff members to fifteen, then to twenty, and the number of staff members kept growing as time went on.

This was a great opportunity for me. After three years on the job, I rose to Senior Probation Officer, a semi-supervisory position. After several more years, I was promoted to Principal Probation Officer II, a Unit Supervisor. Several years later, I was promoted to Principal Probation Officer I, a Division Head, and ultimately to Assistant Chief Probation Officer.

During these years, I had the opportunity to gain a complete overview of the workings and operation of the Criminal Justice System. I worked in both the juvenile and adult supervision units. In addition, I supervised staff working in the Community Service Unit, the Family Unit dealing with child support, municipal services, collections, and intense supervision, and numerous other special units and assignments.

Although I had not majored in Criminal Justice, I was educated by the experience. An additional knowledge-builder in the criminal justice system was working with so many related agencies, to include: judges, prosecutors, investigators, sheriff's officers, local police officers, state police, parole officers, probation officers, corrections officers, private security, and many others. This interaction and exposure added significantly to my educational development and my understanding of the system. Criminal justice personnel also interact with a vast number of social workers, psychologists, counseling agencies, and local schools.

My human relations and interaction skills were further developed and enhanced by my initial position in the criminal justice system. In addition, my entry-level job provided me with networking opportunities, which were a strong base for further advancements and opportunities.

During the early 1970s, the federal government initiated the LEEP (Law Enforcement Educational Program). This was enacted in a multimillion-dollar federal grant that provided funding for any individual employee working in the criminal justice system to pursue further education. The federal government would pay the full tuition as long as the individual maintained a grade-point average of C or better and remained with the agency for three years after obtaining an advanced degree. This was a great opportunity! The grant also provided money to law enforcement and criminal justice agencies to purchase equipment and technology to reduce crime.

The goal of the LEEP grant was to further professionalize and improve the criminal justice system. For me, it meant an opportunity to attend graduate school in the evenings. It should be noted that Criminal Justice was just being developed as a major in colleges and universities. Many institutions of higher learning did not offer a major specifically in Criminal Justice, but some had a course or two in the sociology department dealing with crime and/or criminology.

In addition, only certain colleges and universities were processing the federal grant funding. The closest college to Somerville, New Jersey that used LEEP funding was Rider College (now a university) in Lawrenceville—but they did not offer a Criminal Justice major at the time. The most relevant degree to my work in probation at the time was a Master's Degree in Guidance and Counseling in the Educational Graduate Program. At the time, in the early seventies, I was counseling juvenile offenders, so I felt this was an appropriate choice.

I began taking graduate classes in the evenings, Saturdays, and during the summers, and I received my Master's Degree in Education (Guidance and Counseling) from Rider University in 1973. This was a significant accomplishment for me. As I will discuss later, it was a stepping stone in my career that led to further advancement and also made me eligible to teach at the college level.

CHAPTER 3

FURTHER EDUCATIONAL PURSUITS

U pon graduating with a Master's Degree in Education (Guidance and Counseling), I thought about securing an adjunct teaching position in Criminal Justice. I applied and was hired to teach Introduction to Criminal Justice, a three-credit course, at Raritan Valley Community College in Branchburg, New Jersey in 1974.

I thoroughly enjoyed the teaching experience and thought this was something I would like to continue doing on a part-time basis. I believe my teaching and training experience in the United States Army Reserve (1965-1971) had helped prepare me for this kind of job. While in the Army Reserve, I was selected to attend leadership training to become a drill sergeant. A major component of the four-week training was lecturing to Army recruits, using a formal lesson plan. I served in this position during my term in the United States Army Reserves.

During the training year, I taught classes at the Army Reserve Center to other enlistees, and during the two-week summer camp training, I gave classes to new recruits. Military class lectures are extremely organized and detailed. They taught me to be similarly organized when I started teaching in civilian life.

Raritan Valley is one of the most recognized and professional community colleges in the state of New Jersey and the Branchburg location is a multi-acre, landscaped campus. I feel fortunate to have been a faculty member of this college for more than thirty-five years. Teaching at the community college was beneficial for my career development, and it helped prepare me for ultimately teaching on a full-time schedule at Seton Hall University.

I continued teaching at the community college during my employment with the Somerset County Probation Department except for a two-year period beginning in 1982, when I decided to pursue a Ph.D. I researched the various universities offering a Doctorate in Public Administration, looking for a program that was not in the traditional, evening classroom lecture setting.

A college professor suggested the Union Institute and University, which was a non-traditional and fully accredited university. They offered students the opportunity to create their own program, with the guidance of a committee of four doctorate program consultants. The idea was attractive, and it seemed unique in 1983. I would be able to use alternative methods of learning and receive university credits, with the approval of the committee. For example, I attended a two-week training program for upper-level managers at the National Institute of Corrections in Boulder, Colorado, a national training academy for personnel working in the correctional system. After I submitted a research paper based on the training, I was granted three university credits for the program. This is an example of experiential learning, which I feel is a most essential way to become educated in the criminal justice system.

In experiential learning, students can earn credit by attending conferences, giving guest lectures, or completing internships and providing documentation of learning. As long as you can document these experiences and your attendance and convince your committee members that this was comparable to a three-credit college or university course—by submitting a detailed paper for validation—you can gain credit. The final dissertation requirements were similar to a traditional program.

I found this to be an exciting and unique way of earning my doctorate degree. It was also a good match for my lifestyle at that time. I was married with one child and we were expecting a second. Because I worked full time, I didn't feel I could be away from home several nights a week.

I was accepted into the Doctoral program at the Union Institute and University in 1984, majoring in Public Administration with emphasis in Human Resource Development. The program required an initial ten-day residential colloquium. As an applicant, I was required to compose and present what I envisioned my curriculum and dissertation to be. I would be the facilitator of my own program, guided by a committee of four doctoral-level faculty members—and I had the option to select a fifth committee member from my field of study. The program of study would be presented to other Union faculty and new learners for feedback.

This type of program was ahead of the times for the 1980s. It brought to the forefront the message that there are alternative ways to learn and earn college/university degrees other than the traditional classroom setting. Make no mistake—this was not an easier way of attaining a doctorate. One of my committee members described it as "a Herculean task."

Another advantage for me with this alternate method of learning was that it was a year-round program; therefore, I could work as much and as fast as my schedule permitted. I took advantage of weekends, vacation time, and holidays to complete the program as quickly as possible. Another motivating factor for me was that tuition was monthly, so from a financial perspective, I saved money by working fast. The minimum time frame to meet the program requirements was two years; I completed the program in two years and three months.

The title of my dissertation was "Human Resource Development in Probation Administration and Training." At that time, in 1981, there was no formal training for probation officers in New Jersey. The focus of my study was to determine what the major training areas should be for newly hired officers. I conducted a qualitative study using interviews and questionnaires to gather my data. The subjects of the interview were judges, prosecutors, police officers, Criminal Justice professors, social workers, psychologists, and even probationers. Working in the field of probation was extremely helpful, as I possessed a significant network of subjects to draw from.

I graduated in 1986 with a Ph.D. in Public Administration and concentration in Human Resource Development. This was a milestone for both me and my parents. I was a first-generation son of an immigrant who had achieved the highest educational degree possible. Mom and Dad could not have been prouder. I must also say, I couldn't have accomplished this without the encouragement and assistance of my wife and her superior editing and typing skills.

By this time, I was working in a managerial position in the Probation Department. A Ph.D. was not required; however, my new educational credentials would be helpful in later career opportunities. At that time, very few probation personnel in the State of New Jersey—perhaps only two or three—had doctorate degrees.

CHAPTER 4

CRIMINAL JUSTICE CAREER CHANGE

had ascended the career ladder in the Somerset County Probation Department quickly, from Probation Officer to Senior Probation Officer and then to Principal Probation Officer II and then to Principal Officer I.

I had aspirations of being the next Chief Probation Officer. The Chief Probation Officer was retiring, which presented me with the opportunity to achieve that goal. As the application and screening process progressed, I was one of the two finalists.

Somerset County was in a vicinage (district) with Hunterdon and Warren counties. My competition was the former Probation Chief of Hunterdon, and he got the job. He was a colleague of mine. We had worked together in the probation system and had always gotten along well.

As the new Vicinage Chief, he came to Somerset as his base of operations. I was appointed as his

Assistant Vicinage Chief. Although this was a great accomplishment and honor, I was disappointed that I hadn't gotten the Chief position. John Higgins, the new Chief, and I worked together well, sharing responsibilities and duties. We were the same age, and I did not seeing him retiring from that position any time soon.

I was still teaching at Raritan Valley Community College. As time went on, I seemed to enjoy the teaching more and more. I began to also teach as an adjunct professor at Kean University and the Graduate Department at Seton Hall University. I began to seriously consider retiring from probation and teaching full time. I believed that, with more than twenty-five years of experience working in the field, plus possession of a Ph.D. and teaching experience, I would quickly be offered a full-time position.

I found teaching to be a satisfying profession. I was in a position to share my twenty-nine years of experience in criminal justice with the next generation of practitioners entering the field. I was in the position to mentor students and was perceived as their role model, which was rewarding. I had progressed as much as possible in my present position and I felt it was time for a change.

I started sending out resumes to most colleges in New Jersey, New York, and Pennsylvania within a thirty-five-mile radius. Much to my surprise, I found there were a large number of applicants for these positions. The competition was tough. Finally, after about nine months of searching, I was offered a one-year, temporary position in the

Graduate Department of Public Administration at Seton Hall University. At that time, they offered a Criminal Justice concentration in their Masters in Public Administration program.

I was faced with a difficult decision: Should I retire from a secure government career where there seemed to be no room for advancement to take a one-year, temporary job doing something I might love more? I tossed and turned through a number of sleepless nights, contemplating the choice. I had been working for the government long enough to qualify for an early pension. Adding the pension to the teaching job pay, I could match my yearly salary with the government.

One factor stood out: It had been hard work to get this job offer. I was not a young Ph.D. applicant at the time I was applying for full-time teaching positions. I was fifty-three years old, and I felt that if I did not accept the one-year, non-tenured position at that time, I might not have an opportunity again in the near future.

In August of 1996, I retired from the Somerset County Probation Department and began teaching at Seton Hall University. I strongly believe that having served on the university's Department Advisory Board as well as having numerous contacts with related criminal justice agencies had helped me get this job. I had also served as an adjunct teacher in that department.

The new position required me to teach three graduate courses and also assist in marketing their program. As part of my marketing responsibilities, I gave presentations to potential students contemplating applying to Seton Hall. I also visited police and corrections academy personnel to summarize the curriculum and encourage them to apply to our university. I felt confident speaking in front of groups because of my lecture experience in the military. Marketing seemed natural for me, as I had majored in business marketing as an undergraduate.

The first year sped by, and I was happy to receive a second, one-year appointment—but I was warned that if enrollments did not increase, the position would not be renewed.

Fortunately, a Criminal Justice teaching position became available in the Undergraduate Arts and Sciences Department. I had known the chair of that department from the Criminal Justice Educators Association of New Jersey. He encouraged me to apply, and I decided to do it, since I knew it was likely my present position would be terminated at the end of the academic year. After completing a screening and interviewing procedure, I was hired for the teaching position. It was the beginning of an eighteen-year career with that department.

Working and teaching in a university full time was significantly different from working part time as an adjunct. In addition to teaching, full-time faculty were expected to be active in university committees, to attend department meetings, and to continue their own professional development in their fields of study. Faculty members also were expected to attend new student orientations and discuss the department's program of study.

These orientations usually were on weekends, and occurred numerous times during the year.

Full-time faculty members were required to maintain a caseload of advisees. The number of students might vary, depending on the discipline. At one time, I had sixty-five students to advise. In addition to teaching, all faculty members were required to offer at least four office hours, outside of their classroom hours, for students who might have concerns or questions. Faculty members were expected to attend and participate in state and national conferences related to their discipline. Volunteering for service to the university—such as assisting with research projects or new programs the university was considering—was also expected.

But I had no problem adjusting to this new work environment. I usually worked well with colleagues and was considered a team player. I possessed good interpersonal skills, which had been enhanced early on when I worked in the family business.

Because I was the newest member in the Criminal Justice Department, I was assigned to a number of courses that other faculty chose not to teach. These classes would not have been my preference, but I didn't complain. I felt that accepting these classes would broaden my knowledge and secure my position in the department. For example, the "Statistical Research Methods" class was clearly not within my area of interest or expertise. However, I had to teach that course, because junior faculty had to teach courses assigned by the chairperson.

During my twenty years at Seton Hall, I taught more than twenty different courses— a higher number than any other faculty member in most departments at the university. I taught courses as elementary as "Introduction to Criminal Justice" as well as more in-depth courses, such as "Criminological Theory." During my tenure at the university, I also continued as an adjunct at Rutgers University, New Brunswick, New Jersey and Raritan Valley Community College, Somerville, New Jersey.

I felt I had finally found my niche in the working world—teaching and guiding students in their educational development. Although I certainly had enjoyed my career in criminal probation and believe I had made a positive difference in many peoples' lives, teaching was a new and rewarding career. As I reflect back on my careers, I have no regrets about choosing this career path.

CHAPTER 5

GOVERNOR'S APPOINTMENTS

Before I retired from the Somerset County Probation Department, I wanted to be considered for a governor's appointment to the New Jersey State Parole Board. The role of a parole board member is to evaluate each prisoner who is eligible to be considered for early release from incarceration. Two board members interview the prisoner and decide whether he or she should be released or whether the prisoner should remain in prison, pending another review at a later date.

Board members are similar to judges in relation to their decision-making. The position I was interested in securing was as an alternate board member who is called in when a full-time member was either on vacation or out with an illness. I felt this would be an enhancement to my teaching and believed that I could make a positive contribution to the correctional system in this way, utilizing my education and my experience in criminal justice.

But it takes more than just education and experience to receive an appointment to a parole board. Politics can have a significant effect on appointments. At that time (1999), the Governor was Christine Todd Whitman. I had known Governor Whitman professionally, as she was a former freeholder (New Jersey's term for county board members) in Somerset County, where I worked. In addition to submitting my resume to the Governor's Office, I was endorsed by a State Senator, a Congressman, and a Superior Court Judge.

Shortly after I began teaching at Seton Hall University, I received a call from the governor's office inquiring if I was still interested in the parole board position. I replied that I was. In July, 1999, I received my appointment. This was a great honor, as I was the first alternate parole board member appointed.

I could now pursue and work in two areas of criminal justice that were among my long-term goals, but it meant I had to balance two very important positions. Full-time faculty members are usually not required to teach five days a week; three or four days a week is the norm. My schedule at that time was three days a week. My arrangement with the Parole Board was that I could be available only on the days I did not have classes.

Being on the Parole Board required additional training in the procedures and legal issues relating to this position. The fact that I had worked in the criminal justice system for numerous years made the transition to this new position more comfortable.

During my six years as a member of the board, I interviewed more than four thousand incarcerated individuals. This was an awesome responsibility. I had to help decide, as a member of a two-person panel, who should be released from prison and who should not. We weighed a number of factors. Who was still at risk—and who was not considered to be a risk—of further criminal behavior?

Although this was not a perfect science, I believed I could make this decision fairly, based upon my many years evaluating offenders in the probation system. As a Parole Board member, I was assisted in making this decision by a number of salient factors, to include each inmate's prior record, court documents, police reports, pre-sentence reports, psychological reports, risk assessments, reports on adjustment while incarcerated, and other pertinent information, in addition to the personal interview. The decision I had to make regarding their release or further incarceration is what one may call, "an educated prediction."

This, I believe, is what judges, psychologists, and others who make life-altering decisions must do. They usually decide based upon social and psychological assessments. In the last twenty-five years, researchers have developed risk assessment instruments that can statistically arrive at a score, which normally indicates a range of low, medium, or high risk. We used similar instruments to predict each inmate's propensity for future criminal behavior. These scores are normally based on studies on a large number of individuals as part of a sample population. It has been estimated that such scores are approximately 80 percent reliable. Another means of evaluating an individual's risk of further criminal activity is by conducting a face-to-face interview. This tends to be a more qualitative, but nonetheless invaluable, means of evaluating an individual. I have found, through my experience, that people who have worked in the field of criminal justice—especially interviewing those under investigation—for a significant number of years can more accurately predict future behavior, as compared to those without that experience. Clearly, educational and clinical training are major factors in predicting behavior. Therefore, the combination of training, education, and significant experience working in human behavior fields produces the most accurate results.

Governor's Transition Team

Several months before a governor takes office, a "transition team" is formed. The purpose of this team—which is comprised of ten individuals—is to make recommendations to the incoming governor about major issues facing the state.

Transition teams are formed for all major state departments. I was honored to be appointed to the Transition Team for the Corrections Department prior to Governor Chris Christie's term. This was a non-paid, volunteer committee. All members on the team possessed a significant amount of experience in the field of criminal justice, to include law enforcement, corrections, probation, and social services.

Our task, over several months of meetings, was to summarize in a ten-page "white paper" the recommendations about how major issues facing corrections might be addressed. A chair of the committee was appointed whose responsibility to facilitate the meetings and record the group consensus on the major issues. Our recommendations were then submitted to the governor's office several weeks prior to his swearing in.

It was a great honor and learning experience for me to have this opportunity to interact with a number of accomplished professionals from my field. The contacts I made through this volunteer work were invaluable to me later in my career. In addition, the white paper submitted would have a significant impact on the decision-making of the correctional system in New Jersey.

Reappointment to the Parole Board

In June 2016, I was again appointed to the New Jersey State Parole Board by Governor Chris Christie. It was a great honor to have been appointed to this board by two different governors. When I received this appointment, I decided to retire from Seton Hall University. I had just completed twenty years as a full-time professor. This was the second career from which I retired.

I had enjoyed teaching and mentoring students and therefore, in addition to my parole board work, I decided to accept positions as an adjunct professor at Rider University and Raritan Valley Community College. I was pleased to be hired at Rider University, as that was where I had received my master's degree.

I had taught for more than thirty-five years at Raritan Valley Community College and was honored to continue teaching there, also.

CHAPTER 6

CHANGES IN THE CRIMINAL JUSTICE SYSTEM

Law Enforcement:

As I reflect upon my fiftieth year working in the criminal justice system, I have observed and experienced a number of significant changes. Law enforcement has become more professional in the past fifty years. The requirements to become a police officer still vary from county to county and state to state, but more departments are requiring applicants to have four-year college degrees or college credits. Even if the department does not require college, applicants possessing college credits probably will be given priority.

The training at the police academies has increased and covers more areas than it did in the past. Prospective officers train in combating terrorism and hate crimes; they also receive training in diversity, community policing, and other topics.

The pool of applicants in many areas has increased significantly as policing has become a sought-after career choice for many young adults. It should be noted that demographics can affect this.

There are several reasons young people compete for these positions. Salary levels have increased significantly; the average annual salary for a police officer in New Jersey is $90,000. Many applicants find policing to be an exciting and interesting career. Applicants also may be drawn to making a commitment and might feel a sense of duty to the community and the public.

But law enforcement has come under a lot of scrutiny recently. In addition, because of the events of the past several years, police in some areas may be "targeted" by certain individuals and groups. This is very concerning and has caused what might be called the "Ferguson Effect" in which police nationwide can become hesitant to execute their arrest powers.

It is more imperative than ever that law enforcement authorities be vigilant about their surroundings. It is also important that citizens assist law enforcement by volunteering in meaningful ways, especially by reporting crimes they see ("If you see something, say something!") Citizens also can volunteer to assist in their local police departments by helping with administrative and record-keeping duties.

The 1960s represented a critical and divisive time in our country. President John F. Kennedy and civil rights leader Martin Luther King were assassinated. We were fighting a war in Vietnam while at home, people were demonstrating in favor of civil rights. Many college students were demonstrating on campuses to oppose the war and the military draft. All males age eighteen and over were required to register for the draft; if you were eighteen, able-bodied, and not attending school full-time, there was a good chance you would be drafted and sent to the war zone.

A significant number of soldiers were being injured and killed in the war, and many citizens were not in favor of this conflict. The police were summoned to control and disperse crowds at demonstrations. Law enforcement, in many situations, used aggressive tactics to control demonstrators, to include water hoses, dogs, physical restraint, and other means. A large number of people were arrested.

Because of law enforcement's crowd-control tactics, some protesters were severely injured, as were some police officers. In addition, many students were expelled from their universities for participating in the demonstrations. If they were arrested and convicted, they left school with a criminal record which could preclude them from various professions.

Since the '60s, the methods police use to manage protests and demonstrations has improved significantly. Over the years, law enforcement officers have been trained in crowd control with less use of physical force. You normally don't see the water hoses, dogs, and baton-wielding police controlling crowds at today's demonstrations.

In addition, many police officers now possess some higher education, which can lead to better decision-making.

If one looks at the many demonstrations that take place today in New York City, for example, you may find that there have been few arrests. Police there are using less aggressive methods to control crowds. Procedures and policies will always vary from department to department and state to state.

Community Supervision—Probation and Parole:

There are approximately seven and one-half million people under correctional supervision in the United States. Our country incarcerates a higher percentage of citizens than any other country. About three million people are on probation, two million are on parole, and two-and-one-half million are incarcerated.

Probation is a sentencing alternative after conviction, used in lieu of jail or prison. Probation offers a number of advantages for non-violent and less dangerous individuals. First, a convicted criminal on probation has the opportunity to maintain his or her employment or schooling and to remain in the community. Second, the individual can access rehabilitation through counseling without the stigma of jail or prison. Third, probation is less expensive than housing an inmate. It costs about four thousand dollars per year to maintain a person on probation, as compared to forty thousand dollars yearly to keep someone in prison—and this cost escalates as the inmate ages, due to health and medical needs increasing. Most research also indicates that convicts on probation have a lower rate of recidivism (becoming a repeat offender) compared to those returning to society from prison.

It should be noted, however, that public safety is the overall goal of the correctional system, and people on probation can commit crimes more easily than those who are incarcerated. Today's probation officers are better educated and trained than they were when I entered the field fifty years ago. In addition to a four-year college degree, many possess a master's degree or have plans to pursue one. Additional, ongoing training is available in many departments.

Modern probation officers are better equipped than they were years ago. They often use computers and laptops in their cars, in addition to the pepper spray and bullet-proof vests that normally are provided for law enforcement officers in many jurisdictions. Resources will, again, vary from department to department.

The cooperation and interaction among police officers, sheriff's officers, and parole officers has increased significantly in many places. The future appears to be promising, as the criminal justice system heads toward deinstitutionalizing the present prison population. The federal correctional system has drastically reduced their prison population in the past year, and a number of states are following suit. New Jersey has reduced their prison population in the past ten years from 32,000 to approximately 20,000, by using alternatives to incarceration.

Many citizens in the public sector tend to confuse probation and parole. Parole is the early release of an incarcerated individual based upon satisfactory adjustment and low risk of reoffending. The similarity between probation and parole is that they both supervise persons while they reside in society. A major difference is that a parolee has committed a more serious charge (usually a felony offense) and warrants incarceration.

The guidelines for parole eligibility vary from state to state. In New Jersey, for example, after an inmate has served one-third of his or her sentence—minus "good time" credits (several days credit for each month of good behavior)—they can be considered for parole. They must be interviewed by two parole board members who will review a file containing their charges, prior record, police reports, reasons for sentencing, psychological reports, risk assessment reports, program participation, and any other pertinent information.

Based upon this information and a face-to-face interview, a decision is made to either parole the individual or to deny parole. If denied, the individual will be scheduled for another hearing at a future date, based upon a mathematical formula. The inmate also will be advised about what can be done to improve the chances of receiving parole at the next hearing.

This process is continued until the inmate reaches his or her maximum sentence. If the inmate is granted parole, the board members may attach specific conditions that he or she must satisfy while under supervision, such as attending counseling. The individuals who are released on parole will be supervised by field parole officers carrying caseloads of as many as sixty people.

When I returned to my state's parole board in 2016, I noticed there had been changes in a number of areas. There now was an in-house, two-week training program for all newly appointed board members. A number of the forms had been improved to clarify reasons that an individual was denied parole or granted parole. Board members were now encouraged, in addition to check-off items, to add qualitative remarks to further justify their decisions.

An attorney for the board would review many of the completed forms for legal purposes, in the event the inmate appealed the decision. Clearly, there was an increased scrutiny of the decisions. This was necessary because an inmate could appeal the board members' decision to an appellant review board.

The field-supervising parole officer has the responsibility of enforcing the conditions imposed by the two parole board members upon the prisoner's early release. The officer will supervise, counsel, and attempt to ensure the parolee's satisfactory and positive return to society. They will be responsible for carrying a caseload, the size of which varies from jurisdiction to jurisdiction, depending on budgets, crime rates in the area, and even politics.

Parole officers in New Jersey are also law enforcement officers. They attend an academy similar to police and carry a firearm; the state determined about ten years ago that the training and weapon were needed for safety reasons. However, there have been very few instances where a weapon was needed.

Corrections:

Jails and prisons are presently under significant review. The old philosophy of "lock them up and throw away the key" has generally been ineffective in reducing the overall crime rate. In fact, in many cases, people who are incarcerated become more criminalized. Recidivism rates are approximately 60 percent for those released from prison.

Alternatives to confinement, specifically for those who have committed non-violent crimes, are considered a more appropriate alternative. Prison alternatives may include halfway houses, electronic monitoring, drug courts, mental health courts, daytime reporting centers, ISP (Intense Supervision Probation), and other "diversionary" programs.

For incarcerated individuals, re-entry into society is of paramount importance. The most successful re-entry programs begin while the inmate is still incarcerated. Programs such as drug and alcohol counseling, anger management training, parenting skills, behavior modification, and even college courses may help prepare inmates for finding employment once released. The programs and training available to inmates vary from institution to institution and state to state.

The correction officer in a jail or prison has one of the most challenging jobs in the criminal justice system. They are in an institution with a diverse population ranging from low-risk to high-risk offenders. A significant number of inmates may have mental health issues. The correction officers have to be security officers but also counselors, mentors, father figures, mother figures, and therapists, as well as fulfilling many other roles.

The position of corrections officer does not require a college degree; the minimum requirement is a high school diploma, although in recent years, more applicants have had some college or even four-year degrees. A number of wardens and superintendents now possess college degrees and some have post-graduate degrees.

Their training consists of attending an academy, similar to a police officer's training. In addition, they must possess a valid driver's license and must pass a physical and psychological exam.

Most undergraduate Criminal Justice students do not strive for the position of correction officer, although the salaries, benefits, and retirement packages are comparable to other government positions. Even if one does not want to make a career of this position, it is a great stepping stone to other criminal justice positions, particularly law enforcement. At this time, there is a distinct need for additional female correction officers.

While I was teaching a Corrections course at Seton Hall University several years ago, a female undergraduate student told me she wanted to complete an internship at a county jail. The internship required the student to work in the jail, under supervision, for one hundred and fifty hours during the semester. In addition, she was required to complete a research paper and meet periodically with the internship coordinator.

The student performed exceptionally well and received high marks from her jail supervisor. Upon completing the internship and graduating from the program, she applied for a full-time, paid position at the jail. She was hired and is still working there as of this writing. Administration at the jail is very impressed with her performance, and I anticipate that she will be considered for a supervisory position in the near future. I have invited her back on several occasions as a guest speaker in my undergraduate classes, so that my new students can see her as a role model for that position.

CHAPTER 7

TIPS FOR SUCCESS FOR CRIMINAL JUSTICE APPLICANTS

I cannot emphasize enough the importance of networking, as often as possible, with individuals and agencies in related criminal justice agencies and organizations.

When I worked in the probation department in Somerset County, our offices were located in the county complex, which also housed the courts, the county prosecutors' offices, the Sheriff's Department, and other county departments. Each day when I finished my lunch, I walked around the complex and tried to meet and talk with other related criminal justice personnel. By doing this, I met and formed relationships with a number of people working in these departments. In my experience, face-to-face meetings are much more effective than getting to know people through e-mail or correspondence. To this day, I still maintain contact with many of these individuals.

It's also helpful to join criminal justice organizations. Every discipline or career has professional organizations. Examples in the criminal justice field include the American Correction Association, Probation and Parole, Criminal Justice Educators, and the American Jail Association, to name a few. I strongly recommended that you not only join several professional organizations, but also become actively involved as an organization's officer or committee member. The contacts and possible employment opportunities you will find through these organizations can be invaluable. In addition, stay on their mailing lists, because the literature you receive will keep you current in the field. You want to be as informed as possible about a career position you are seeking.

Make the most of your time as an undergraduate student. I have found that students who are engaged during classroom lectures are most successful. I base these recommendations on a qualitative analysis of more than six thousand students at a number of different colleges and universities where I have lectured.

1. **Sit in the front**. Students who sit toward the front or middle of the classroom seem to do better scholastically than those who sit in the back or corners.

2. **Be prepared**. Students who are prepared from the initial class seem to do better. This includes having the text for the class and reviewing the syllabus before the first day of class, and taking notes every day.

3. **Rest up**. Students who come to class well-rested are usually more alert and receptive to information being discussed.

4. **Participate**. Students who participate on a regular basis usually do well in class. Volunteer to respond to the professor's inquiries and ask relevant questions regarding the subject matter.

5. **Do your homework**. Students who complete and submit their assignments when or before they are due—according to the class syllabus—often place in the upper range of the class.

6. **Show up for class**. Attending classes on a regular basis is a great advantage to students. It is impossible to do your best in a class if you miss a number of lectures.

7. **Interact with your professor**. Students who get to know their professors and discuss relevant issues with them, even after class or during office hours, normally get better grades.

8. **Network**. Students who get to know a number of their classmates, through study groups or informally, usually perform at a higher level than those who do not.

9. **Join professional clubs or associations**. Attending meetings will enhance your knowledge and contacts in this discipline.

10. **Keep reading**. Students who seek outside, related reading material on the topics addressed in class will enhance their knowledge and perspective on the subject.

Internships can also unlock doors for students who want to find work in the criminal justice field. An internship provides the student with real-life experiences working alongside full-time criminal justice employees and can help establish a useful network.

While working at Seton Hall University, I served as an internship coordinator for students majoring in Criminal Justice. I worked in conjunction with the school's career center to encourage students to experience an internship and also assist them in securing a placement that was appropriate for them and their career choice. I recruited additional criminal justice agencies within New Jersey and neighboring states to participate in this program by joining the pool of agencies offering internships.

Internships can provide a number of significant advantages. Working alongside criminal justice employees can help each student decide whether the field is a good "fit." In some cases, they may conclude that this is not really the right career position for them, which allows them to begin to focus their resources and attention elsewhere. If they find the internship exciting, they may decide to apply to the same agency upon graduation, and having already served as an intern can give the applicant a distinct advantage over other applicants.

Some internships are paid, which helps defray the student's expenses. If a student registers for an internship through their college or university and meets certain requirements, they can also receive college credits toward their degree. Each college or university sets the criteria and requirements. The internship experience also gives students network contacts and something to list on their resume. If an internship isn't available or practical, students can also volunteer with an agency of their choice, although they usually will receive no formal college credits for a volunteer position.

Career fairs are an excellent way for a student to meet representatives from various criminal justice agencies. Most colleges and universities will host at least one career fair during the academic year. Students who attend can learn about hiring procedures, working conditions, and salaries at each agency, plus make an initial contact with each agency that is a potential job source.

If you are sincere about applying to a particular agency for employment upon graduation, dress professionally and bring a current resume. A number of students I worked with over the years ended up securing a position through a contact they made at a career fair. Research any agency you plan to talk with at the fair and be prepared to ask some relevant questions, which will usually impress the agency representative. At the end of your conversation, get the representative's contact card. The next day, send or e-mail a short follow-up note regarding your interest in the agency and thanking them for their time.

If your college or university offers a Criminal Justice major or minor, make it a point to get to know your professor during his or her office hours, in addition to in the classroom. Many have had direct experience working in the field and might have pursued related research that they are willing to share with you. They can provide the student with helpful advice regarding a career in criminal justice. During my twenty years of full-time teaching, I found it surprising how rarely students came in during my office hours to discuss their status in the classroom or career opportunities. I noticed that those who dropped by my office with questions and inquiries usually fared better academically and were more successful in securing internships and even jobs.

The vast majority, if not all, colleges and universities have a career center. Career centers can provide significant resources in a number of important areas. They can help students prepare for interviews and create resumes, and they often know about available internships and career positions. In my experience, most students do not take full advantage of their career center resources, even though they are paying for this service through their tuition! Career centers normally assign a career counselor for each discipline. It can be most beneficial for the student to make an appointment with this counselor early in their college years, because the counselor can be of great assistance in meeting career goals.

Students preparing for a career in criminal justice must ask themselves: "How am I qualified differently than other graduating criminal justice majors? What skills, experience, or other qualities make me a more desirable candidate than others?" Certifications can be helpful here. Certifications in first aid, emergency management, water safety, sign language, drug counseling, and many other fields can make a candidate more attractive to a prospective employer. Speaking a second language or having exceptional technical and computer skills also can be a major advantage. Acquiring these skills and certifications can enhance a student's chances of being selected for a position.

Keep a portfolio of documentation when you attend any criminal justice-related conferences, workshops, or training. Maintain copies of your certifications and credits as evidence that you participated. Remember, you must market yourself! It's much easier to do so when your paperwork is in order.

CHAPTER 8

WAYS TO SECURE EMPLOYMENT IN CRIMINAL JUSTICE

There are a number of ways applicants may seek employment in criminal justice.

1. **Civil Service Tests**: Civil service examinations are the first step to a vast number of positions in government and criminal justice. This exam may be required for positions in law enforcement, probation, parole, corrections, and others. Applicants with the highest scores are often the first considered for these positions.

Civil service exams are offered periodically; the times, dates, and locations will be listed on government websites. The exams are objective and are designed to not discriminate against gender, religion, or ethnic backgrounds. Prepare for a civil service exam by reviewing publications that list previous questions from civil service exams, which can be found at libraries and bookstores. You also might want to hire a private tutor or enroll in study-preparation seminars. Many criminal justice organizations also will require the applicant to undergo a psychological evaluation prior to being hired.

2. **Chief's Test**: This is an exam created by an individual police department for applicants. Study guides can be found for these kinds of exams, and it's also possible to use a private tutor or enroll in a training seminar prior to the test. Those with the highest scores will usually be interviewed and might be asked to undergo a psychological screening or even submit a writing sample. Applicants also will be asked to supply a number of references.

3. **Appointed Positions**: There are several appointing authorities (the President, Governor, Prosecutor, etc.) who appoint individuals directly to various positions. A number of upper-level positions in government and criminal justice are filled by direct appointments. The position of United States Marshal for New Jersey is appointed by the President of the United States. The positions of Superior Court Judge, County Prosecutor, and Chairman of the State Parole are examples of direct appointments also sometimes made by governors. The selection of persons for these positions will vary from state to state.

It should be noted that an appointment to this type of position might not have long-term security. As administrations change politically, the appointing authority may decide to appoint a different individual to the position. Unfortunately, sometimes qualifications for the job are secondary to politics.

I believe that, if you are offered an appointed position, it is advantageous to accept. The number of influential people you will interact with might prove very helpful as you seek other employment in the field, even if you are not reappointed.

4. **Elected Positions**: Some criminal justice positions are filled by the electoral process. Voters go to the polls and vote for a candidate of their political affiliation. For example, in some states, voters can choose judges and prosecutors. In New Jersey, each county's sheriff is chosen through an election every three years. There are twenty-one counties in New Jersey, and therefore twenty-one sheriffs. These kinds of elected positions tend to be quite politically oriented, although hopefully, qualifications also are a factor. Each potential sheriff begins campaigning months before his or her term expires. In many cases, those who assist in the sheriff's campaign will be given a position in the new sheriff's administration. As previously indicated, there may not be much job security if the present official is not reelected.

5. **Temporary Positions**: Sometimes criminal justice agencies hire an individual temporarily, pending the outcome of a formal testing procedure. This normally occurs when an agency needs an immediate replacement and does not have the time to wait until an exam is scheduled, advertised, given, and graded. In fact, this is how the author of this book was hired for a temporary position in the probation system. An employee resigned and created an immediate need to cover a caseload of offenders, and probation officials didn't want

to wait to schedule the civil service exam. I was hired with the understanding that, if I did not pass the civil service exam with a high enough score, I would be dismissed. However, in many cases, if an individual is hired on a temporary basis and then does not score sufficiently high enough on the exam, they may be offered an alternate position in the agency.

I encountered a similar situation when I was teaching at Seton Hall University. A chief probation officer that I knew called me one day and indicated that there was an immediate need for a bi-lingual probation officer, but it would be a temporary position. He inquired if I had any graduating college seniors who were fluent in Spanish. I gave him a list of students who possessed that skill, and he selected one of my students for the position. I maintained contact with that student, and she indicated that she later passed the civil service exam with a high enough score and was hired on a permanent basis.

Sometimes temporary positions are related to the grants an agency receives. A temporary position might be created for a specific project, and the applicant is hired with the understanding that the position might be eliminated when funding runs out. As I have witnessed over the years, in many situations, an individual who performs in an excellent manner during his or her temporary term will be offered an alternate position if funding disappears.

6. **Special Skills**: Special skills, certifications, credentials, licenses, or talents can enhance your employability. Most organizations are seeking

the most qualified and experienced individual for their agency, but they also might be influenced by fluency in another language, special licenses such as a pilot's license, qualification in various levels of first-aid, excellent technical computer and programming skills, etc. Maintain copies of documents proving your additional skills or certifications. Advanced educational degrees are usually advantageous, even if they are not a requirement of the position. Further educational pursuits normally indicate motivation and perseverance to a potential employer.

7. **Positive Interviewing**: After the preliminary testing or examination for a position in criminal justice, most agencies will require an in-person interview. The interview is an opportunity to sell yourself to the organization. It is strongly recommended that an applicant practice interviewing in advance. This can be accomplished in several ways. Career centers at colleges and universities often offer workshops on interviewing that might include practice interviews. You can also practice being interviewed by a friend or family member.

You might choose to have someone videotape the interview and then critique it. The more you practice, the more comfortable you will feel during the real interview. Some sample questions a potential employer might ask include:

- Why should we hire you?
- What special talents or skills can you contribute to our organization?
- What do you expect to be doing five years from now?

- What are your strengths?
- What are your weaknesses?

8. **Network-Network-Network**: I've written this before, but it cannot be emphasized enough: Networking can be of significant importance in helping you secure a position in criminal justice. Let your friends, neighbors, colleagues, family, professors, priest, etc. know you are now seeking a career position. You never know who may have valuable information that can assist you. People in your network might also be able to provide you with information about another resource, agency, or person who can assist in your goals.

Here's an example about a colleague of mine who was seeking a position in state government and how he achieved his goal. When a new governor was elected, my colleague began attending mass every Sunday in the same house of worship the governor attended. He decided to bring his resume to church one day, and at the end of mass, he quickly handed it to the governor. This is clearly a non-traditional means of submitting one's resume. However, several weeks later, he received a telephone call from the governor's office and was scheduled for an interview. He was subsequently offered an administrative position on the governor's staff. I certainly am not recommending this strategy as a means to secure a position, but it helps me emphasize that using all resources and creativity can be beneficial.

It is also helpful to create your own "bank" of contacts. A good starting point is to request and collect business cards from everyone you meet who is connected with the field you are interested in. Most people you meet at conferences, seminars, and workshops will be happy to provide you with their contact information.

When seeking a career position in criminal justice, it is beneficial to have a first, second, and third choice of positions. For example, if your first choice is to become an F.B.I. agent, perhaps your second choice would be a state trooper, and your third choice a local police officer. It would great if your first choice offered you a position, but if they do not, at least you have a back-up plan.

It is important that you "market yourself." You should not be embarrassed to "blow your own horn." If you have published an article, received an award, served on an advisory board, or made some other important contribution to your discipline, let the potential employer know. List it in your resume and mention it during you interview. Remember, you want to distinguish yourself from all the others who are seeking the same position.

CHAPTER 9

PROFESSIONAL DEVELOPMENT

s I was taking my last class in graduate school, I could hardly wait to complete the course and graduate. I thought this would be my last pursuit of formal education. That was enough!

One of my professors observed how eager many of us were to complete the coursework. To this day, I clearly recall his words to us: "Learning is lifelong, from cradle to grave." Many of us did not pay too much attention to this statement at that time. Ironically, several years after graduating with my master's degree, I returned to pursue my doctorate. By the time I received my Ph.D., I completely understood the philosophy of lifelong learning. I now believe that, as long as we are alive, we must continue to learn.

If you can afford the time and money to pursue further formal education, you will find it is a benefit, personally and professionally. A higher educational degree can be the deciding factor in securing your desired goals. If, for financial reasons, you cannot afford the cost of further education, you can still increase your knowledge both generally and specifically in your discipline and career. These are some examples of alternate means of attaining additional information and education in criminal justice.

Most career criminal justice agencies are affiliated with one or more professional organizations. Many of these organizations host annual conferences presenting various workshops in the field. As a member, you can attend and even receive credits by participating in certain workshops. What you learn will make you better informed and educated in your field, and you will meet individuals to add to your network of contacts.

Most professional organization publish a monthly or quarterly newsletter or periodical full of information about current issues, laws, trends, and changes in their discipline. You can expand your education by reading these periodicals. Many professional organizations will offer, at no cost, online seminars regarding subject matter pertaining to their discipline. Check the professional organization websites for a significant amount of information on a diverse number of subjects related to your career position.

Many colleges and universities have a speakers' bureau that maintains a listing of speakers available to address your organization, usually for no fee. More often than not, these speakers will come to your group or organization to share their expertise.

Police academies in many counties and states may offer, at minimal or no cost, classes or seminars for the public pertaining to subject matter of interest in criminal justice, such as "How to burglar-proof your house" or "First-aid and CPR." Some police academies host "citizens police academy seminars" free of charge for the public. These seminars offer a wealth of information.

The National Institute of Corrections (NIC) is a training academy offering classes, seminars, and research papers on a variety of correctional issues. Those employed in some area of corrections, probation, and parole can apply to attend training at their facility. A limited number of individuals from across the United States, representing a cross-section of the various correctional positions, are selected to attend. If accepted, the applicant's expenses (transportation, lodging, and meals) are paid by NIC. Applicants must agree to share the information they receive with other departments in their home state. The instructors at NIC possess extensive experience in their respective fields. I have been fortunate to have been selected to attend weeklong training events on three occasions during my correctional career.

Other areas in the criminal justice field, such as law enforcement and the courts, also have academic or training institutes. The FBI Academy is a national center offering training relating to law enforcement. The National Center for State Courts (NCSC) offers a variety of courses and seminars relating to the administration of the courts.

Some colleges and universities offer certificate, non-college-credit programs related to criminal justice. These programs are normally of short duration, perhaps five or six classes or seminars, and cover a variety of subjects including management topics, such as major skills and techniques in supervising staff. The attendees will not normally receive a grade and may not even be tested, but they will receive a "certificate of attendance" and gain additional knowledge. Non-credit academic programs are another alternative if you don't have the time and money for a full-semester course, but still want to enhance your knowledge in a specific subject area.

Another way to gain additional knowledge and expertise is to volunteer in an agency or organization about which you would like to learn more. Most agencies will not turn down a non-paid individual who can provide some assistance. For example, let's say you wanted to learn more about the processing of a criminal case from arrest to sentencing. You could contact your local county prosecutor's office and set up an appointment to make this request. Be prepared to explain why you would like to learn about this issue. Indicate your position (such as student or practitioner in a related field) and be sure to say which day or days you would be available to volunteer and the duration of time (weeks, months). This is an excellent way to see the practical aspects of an issue by working with and observing practitioners.

CHAPTER 10

WHERE DO WE GO FROM HERE?

During my years of teaching and working in criminal justice, I have heard comments from both students and the public at large regarding the criminal justice system. Many of the comments were not positive, such as, "The criminal justice system is broken" or "There is no justice."

I disagree that the system is broken. Can it, like any other system, be improved? Yes. The American criminal justice system has been significantly altered and improved in numerous ways in the past fifty years. For example, the trend today is to attempt to reduce the prison population, based upon recognition of the fact that long-term incarceration does not normally reduce recidivism.

In a number of states, the prison population is slowly being reduced. New Jersey is a great example. We have gone from thirty two thousand inmates in the last ten years to approximately twenty thousand. The federal prison system is also reducing its population. In addition, more and more jurisdictions are offering re-entry programs to help prepare the inmate to return to society. More prison systems are offering skills training and educational programs. In fact, some institutions offer college-level courses for certain inmates who qualify.

Many jurisdictions also offer additional alternatives to incarceration such as electronic monitoring, intense supervision programs, halfway houses, therapeutic programs, drug court, mental health court, and veterans court, to name a few.

The bail system has come under renewed scrutiny, and as of January 2017, the system has undergone a major change. Prior to 2017, if two individuals were co-defendants in the commission of a crime, the amount of bail would probably be the same for both, even if one defendant was very wealthy and the other unemployed. This was deemed by the courts to be discriminatory. The revised bail system is now based upon a risk assessment evaluation of both defendants; if the risk score is low enough, they might be released with no monetary bail and simply be monitored by a court services officer until the date of their next court appearance. These are significant changes in the criminal justice system, although it should be noted again that policies and programs vary from state to state.

And what of the common complaint by victims of crimes and others that "There is no justice?" Yes, there is a justice system. One may not always agree with the prosecuting, judging, and sentencing of an individual, but this is our justice system.

Perceptions of justice vary from jurisdiction to jurisdiction. Criminal justice is not a perfect science, but through our appeals system and changes in the laws, the system is always evolving and improving. Administrations and administrators are constantly changing, as tenure in positions change, and the newly appointed managers often possess different philosophies, which helps the system to evolve.

People entering the criminal justice field today are better trained and educated than in the past. The General Electric Corporation had as a slogan many years ago: "People are our most important product." This, I believe, holds true in the criminal justice field today. Good people tend to operate good organizations.

When people or groups do not agree with a law or action, they can be influential in creating change through legislative action, petitions, and political lobbying. Families of victims have had a significant impact on implementing and/or changing laws and programs. An example is Mothers Against Drunk Drivers (MADD), an organization that was initiated by a mother who had lost a daughter due to a drunken driver. Megan's Law, which makes information about sex offenders more available to the public, was initiated by the mother of a young girl who was sexually assaulted and murdered by a sex offender.

Most citizens form their opinions and perceptions of the criminal justice system from media sources such as television and newspapers.

Unfortunately, in many cases, they are not getting the complete and most accurate information. One must review the complete list of facts in order to make an informed judgment.

In order to help clarify the true situation in our criminal justice system, I'd like to discuss a few "Facts and Fictions" about the system.

"Once a criminal, always a criminal": Not true! A significant number of previously convicted individuals have turned their lives around and made valuable contributions to society. One of the goals of a meaningful criminal justice system is rehabilitation, and we are constantly striving to increase the percentage of former criminals who now lead successful lives.

Case studies: Although convicted felons have a high incidence of recidivism—with approximately 60 percent committing further crimes—a number of success stories exist. I know of a felony offender who served seven years in prison and then, upon being released, went on to earn a four-year college degree. He is now pursuing his master's degree in Social Work and is working for a state department of corrections as a counselor for inmates.

Another inmate who was released after serving a significant portion of a life sentence on a murder charge went on to secure his law degree. In addition to his private practice, he now assists other disadvantaged and high-risk individuals on the streets in a high crime area.

Although these cases are exceptional, they illustrate that, if an individual is motivated enough and perseveres enough, he or she can adjust and live successfully in society. Inmates who take advantage of the counseling programs offered in a correctional setting might find it easier to make a positive adjustment. However, if an inmate is not significantly motivated to change a criminal lifestyle, just being incarcerated will not necessarily change his or her life. Unfortunately, prisons expose inmates to a number of negative influences such as gangs and drugs, and some inmates succumb to these.

"Some prisons are like country clubs": This is an exaggeration, for the most part. I am in my fiftieth year working in criminal justice, and I am not aware of any "country club prisons." Are some prisons newer, with improved and modern conditions? Yes. For example, most of the older prisons were not air conditioned. Today, most prisons being built are air conditioned, which creates a more healthful and humane environment for inmates and correctional staff. A comfortable indoor temperature can help reduce the stress level in areas with very hot and humid conditions. One of the main reasons for prison riots, years ago, was poor living conditions within the prison.

Do some prisons offer more open spaces for prisoners to move around in? Yes. Many federal prisons offer a "softer" type of incarceration. This might be because many federal prisoners are "white collar" criminals who may not necessarily be violent or physically dangerous to others and therefore require less security. Much of the mobility and restrictions of an inmate in any institution will be based upon the inmate's risk classification assessment, which determines their placement in the prison setting. But even the most modern, comfortable prison setting is no "country club."

"Being on probation or parole is a slap on the wrist": If administered properly, probation and parole are an intensive and effective form of justice. Inmates who receive probation or parole must adhere closely to the following rules:

1. Must report to the officer as directed.
2. Cannot move to a different address without permission.
3. Must maintain full-time employment or be a full-time student.
4. Must pay all financial assessments.
5. Must refrain from the use of drugs.
6. Must permit the officer to visit them at their residence.
7. Must submit to periodic drug testing.

A judge often also imposes special conditions on the individual who begins probation or parole. A specific curfew can be ordered; the inmate can be commanded to avoid certain geographic areas; or the inmate might be ordered to not associate with or contact any victims of their crime. The judge also might suspend an inmate's driving privileges for a period of time or impose other appropriate restrictions. Failure to follow all the rules imposed can lead to the inmate forfeiting his or her probation or parole and returning to incarceration in prison.

An officer's effectiveness in supervising offenders on probation or parole is often influenced by the number of clients he or she is asked to supervise. An officer given a reasonable caseload of forty to fifty offenders can be successful in monitoring these individuals. If an officer has a caseload of one hundred or more, they will find it more difficult task to assist in each offender's rehabilitation.

Intense Supervision Probation or Parole (ISP) programs often have a higher success rate, because ISP officers carry a caseload of between fifteen and twenty cases and are therefore able to spend more time with their clients. ISP offenders normally are in need of greater supervision and services. Most departments have a small number of ISP officers because of the relatively higher cost of having officers with only fifteen or twenty cases.

"Police use excessive force on a regular basis": Most average citizens receive their information about an incident of excessive police force from media sources such as television, which might not report the complete set of facts. Circumstances that may have preceded the incident might not have been disclosed or videotaped. The reporters involved might not have been Criminal Justice majors who thoroughly understand the process.

When one looks at the number of police officers nationally, the percentage of those found guilty of using excessive force is very small. New York City police has 35,000 police officers, but very few who have been found guilty of using excessive force. Yes, these incidents do happen—but when officers are found guilty, they usually lose their jobs and often have to also serve a prison term.

Personnel employed in the criminal justice system are "held to a higher standard" of conduct by the courts because officers are in a position to uphold the law and use their professional discretion. Of course, there are "the good and the bad" in every profession, but media reports can give viewers the impression that police brutality is common. It is not.

I certainly agree that law enforcement officers should not use force unless it is absolutely necessary. But we must keep in mind that law enforcement officers are human beings possessing emotions and even prejudices. In dangerous and highly emotional situations, they have to make split-second decisions. Their adrenaline may also affect the decision.

The police academy training in most states contains a diverse curriculum including both physical and classroom curriculum. However, no amount of training can cover every possible situation or critical incident that might occur. A chief probation officer who hired me many years ago, after I had passed the civil service test and series of interviews, told me: "Use *common sense* when you are out in the field." I never forgot those words, and I called them to mind many times while I was a field officer.

I feel strongly that the issue of excessive force by law enforcement officers is being addressed today. We are recruiting better-trained and more educated personnel for law enforcement positions. More departments now place cameras on the officers' uniforms and on their patrol cars, making it possible to monitor how they handle every situation. Police academies now offer increased training on the issue of how and when to use force.

As previously mentioned, criminal justice is not a perfect science; however, I am confident, based upon my years in the criminal justice system, that we are regularly reviewing and improving the system to a great extent. We must also keep in mind that criminal justice is also subject to the two factors that always influence government agencies: money and politics.

Criminal justice continues to be an interesting and rewarding career option. It is a relatively new discipline. It was only in the early 1970s that Criminal Justice became a major field of study in colleges and universities. In many institutions of higher learning, Criminal Justice is still not a "stand-alone" department; some schools consider this field part of Sociology, Political Science, Public Administration, or even the Business Department. Only in the past few decades has the field of criminal justice been recognized as a professional career rather than just a "job."

I sincerely believe that the future of this discipline is on a positive, upward trend. One of the most significant issues facing our country at this time is the fight against terrorism. Ever since September 11, 2001, there has been a marked increase in the number of positions created to address safety and security.

Unfortunately, criminal activity and terrorism will continue to be major issues in the foreseeable future. Therefore, we will continue to need dedicated, educated, and well-trained individuals to choose this important career.

I have dedicated the majority of my working career to criminal justice. I plan on continuing my work in this most rewarding field.

SOME CAREER POSITIONS IN CRIMINAL JUSTICE

Careers in Law Enforcement

Customs Canine Enforcement Officer

Customs Import Specialist

Customs Inspector

Customs Patrol Officer

Customs Pilot

Customs Enforcement Agent

Customs Special Agent

Fish and Wildlife Service, Special Agent

Immigration and Naturalization Service, Border Patrol Agent

Immigration and Naturalization Criminal Investigator

Immigration and Naturalization Deportation Officer

Immigration and Naturalization Inspector

Inspector General Investigator

Internal Revenue Criminal Investigator

Deputy U.S. Marshal — Internal Revenue Internal Security Inspector

Drug Enforcement Special Agent — Naval Investigative Service/ Criminal Investigator

Environmental Conservation Special Agent — Park Police (United States)

Federal Bureau of Investigation Special Agent — Postal Service Inspector

Federal Investigations Investigator — Secret Service Agent

Federal Protective Service Officer/Criminal Investigator — Secret Service Uniformed Office

State and Municipal Law Enforcement

County Park Police — Police Officer (Municipal)

Deputy Sheriff — State Police Officer/ State Trooper

Investigator (State, County, Municipal)

Careers in the Courts

Attorney/Lawyer — Pretrial Services Officer, U.S. District Courts

Bailiff (Court Officer) — Probation Officer

Court Administrator — Release-On-Own- Recognizance (ROR) Interviewer

Court Clerk — Research Analyst/ Statistician

Court Liaison Counselor — Support Services Coordinator

Court Reporter (Short-Hand Reporter)	Site Supervisor
Court Representative	Victim Services Personnel:
Court Services Officer	Child and Youth Counselor
Domestic Violence Counselor	Crisis Counselor
Judge	Runaway Counselor
Paralegal/Legal Assistant	Victim Services Specialist

Careers in Corrections

Correctional Treatment Specialist (Federal Prison)	Other Related Corrections Occupations:
Corrections Counselor	Academic Teacher
Corrections Officer	Caseworker/HIV Specialist
Juvenile Justice Counselor	Classification and Treatment Director
Juvenile Probation Officer	Clinical Psychologist
Parole Counselor	Correctional Facilities Specialist
Parole Officer	Education Counselor
Pre-Release Program Correctional Counselor	Facilities Specialist
Pre-Release Program Employment Counselor	Inmate Records Coordinator
Pre-Release Program Halfway House Manager	Management Coordinator
Private Corrections, Corrections Corp. of America; Wackenhut	Penologist
Probation Officer	Prisoner-Classification Interviewer

State Parole Board Member   Recreational Counselor

Warden   Substance Abuse Specialist

Vocational Counselor

Careers in Forensic Science/Criminalistics

Criminalistics: Crime Laboratories:

Arson Specialist   Bureau of Alcohol, Tobacco, and Firearms

Ballistics Specialist   Drug Enforcement Administration

Document Specialist   Federal Bureau of Investigation

Fingerprint Specialist   U. S. Customs Service

Polygraph Specialist

Serology Specialist

Toolmark Specialist

Careers in Private Security

Diverse Employment Opportunities: Job Responsibilities

Commercial Security   Administrator/Manager

Industrial Security   Investigator

Institutional Security   Protective Specialist

Retail Security   Technician

N.B.: It should be noted that job titles may vary from state to state.

Additional Criminal Justice positions in Federal Government may be found at USA.Jobs.Gov

You may contact Dr. Paitakes for any further inquires or discussion at:
e-mail: pait@optonline.net

https://www.facebook.com/50YearsWorkingInCriminalJustice

Twitter handle:
@JohnMPaitakes
www.twitter.com

CPSIA information can be obtained
at www.ICGtesting.com
Printed in the USA
FFOW04n2346091017
40920FF